Becoming Barford

The story of a Warwickshire village

BARFORD HERITAGE GROUP

First published in 2010 by

Barford Heritage Group

www.barfordheritage.org

Copyright © Barford Heritage Group

ISBN   978-0-9565248-0-5

Designed by Martin Nolan

Printed by Warwick Printing Company Limited

Becoming Barford traces the development of the village using pictures and reminiscences. This ancient settlement on a bank of the River Avon has been shaped by dramatic changes over the years; from a Saxon society to one ruled by foreign feudal lords; from the all powerful influence of the Church to the rise, after the Enclosure Act, of powerful secular landowners; from a self-sustaining community with diverse trades yet crippling hardships, to a century suffering two World Wars.

The river

Our story begins with the River Avon which provided the main reason for the settlement being established here in prehistoric times and helps to explain the desirability of Barford as a place to live through the centuries to the present day. For hundreds of years the river was owned by Lords of the Manor of Barford, including the Earls of Warwick. It was used for transport, as a source of power and food (there was once a full time fisherman and a number of part time poachers) and records show that there was a floating garden beside the bridge. Its banks were used for cultivation of willows which were pollarded for basket making and of course the river was used for recreation.

"The River Avon ran through the village, and this was a source of endless delight to us all through the long summer holidays. It was so clear and shallow, fast flowing and beautiful. We paddled and caught minnows, sticklebacks and tiddlers to our hearts' content. We caught them in our hands, and then threw them back again into the waters under the bridge at the Warwick end of the village. At the other end, on the road towards Wasperton village, there was the River Banks, an even more delightful place. The water here was a little deeper and we taught ourselves to swim on bundles of bullrushes under our arms. The river here was narrower and it was a perfect place for a picnic on a hot day."

Barford bridge

It was the Anglo-Saxons who formed the first recognisable community at Barford. At this time much of Mercia would have been woodland which early settlers cleared for use as arable and pasture land. They would have soon discovered they could wade across the river carrying their load of barley at the shallow ford – hence the name 'Barford'. Later, a wooden foot bridge was constructed and, by 1484, there was also a stone bridge. The present bridge dates from the 1700s.

The original settlement would probably have occupied today's Bridge Street and Church Street with farming beginning on the higher ground. Early farmers worked an 'open field system' cultivating scattered, long, narrow strips leaving characteristic 'ridges and furrows' on the landscape. This system was to last for almost another 750 years. In Barford there are many excellent examples of this once cultivated land now being used as pasture.

Lords of the Manor

The Norman invasion of 1066 brought about massive changes as William the Conqueror swept away the Anglo-Saxon past and enforced the French language. Land was taken away from the ruling overlords and given to William's favoured subjects. These early Lords of the Manor imposed a feudal organisation on villagers with 'serfs' at the bottom of the pile.

The first recorded Lord of the Manor was 'Henry de Bereford' who gave the church and much land in Barford to Thelsford Priory. The friars were to become the largest landowners in the village by 1332.

The Domesday survey of 1068, records that there was a mill at Barford worth '2s and 13 sticks of eels', where 'a stick' represented 25 of these nutritious fish. Monks were given the water mill (next to Avonside) which they operated in conjunction with a monastic farm or 'Grange' opposite St Peter's Church. Centuries later, ownership of the mill reverted to the Earls of Warwick who let it to various millers over the years, so we can see that the power of the river has been harnessed to grind corn into flour for many hundreds of years.

Barford entry in the Domesday Book

Successive Lords of the Manor built fine houses, all now gone, but we have a sketch of the last Fairfax manor house demolished in the mid nineteenth century. Generations of the Fairfax family were the largest landowners in the village.

Fairfax Manor

Fairfax Fireback

St Peter's Church

The original thatched, wooden Saxon church of St Peter's was rebuilt about 1200, and there is a list of rectors going back to 1280. The existing tower dates from the 1300s.

Photograph of a portrait of the Rev.ᵈ RICHARD UNETT Rector of Barford 1701-1727. He belonged to an ancient family of gentry. He was born in 1661 (or 5) He gave a chalice, paten and flagon to the Church in 1714. He died 29.ᵗʰ August 1727, aged 66 (or 61).

Buried in Barford Church

Reverend Richard Unett

Photograph of a portrait of Mistress MARY UNETT wife of the Rev.ᵈ Richard Unett. She is said to have been the daughter of John Dodd (or Dod) She appears to have been married to the Rector when he was about 40 and she was about 20, and to have survived him nearly 40 years, dying 11th July

Mary Unett

St Peter's Church before rebuild

Barford Hall

By 1538, when Henry VIII dissolved the monasteries, Thomas Ward bought the site of the Priory Grange and built a magnificent timber-framed house known as Barford Hall. We can see that, even then, Barford had a tenuous Royal connection.

A branch of the Ward family tree

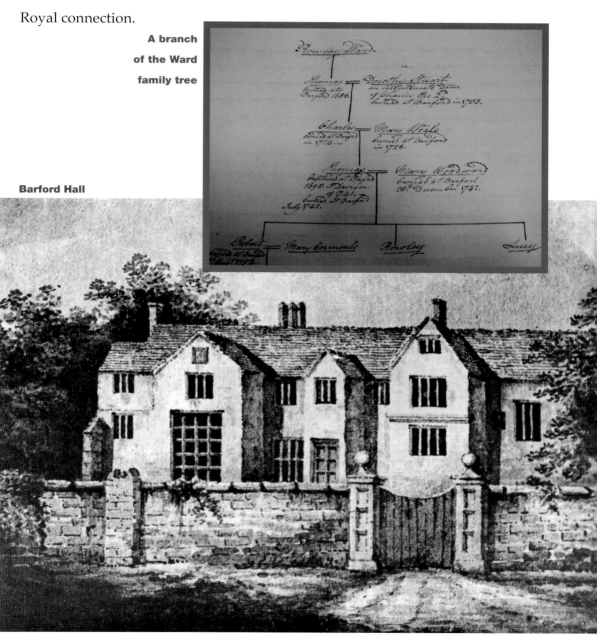

Barford Hall

Barford properties

By this time the northern access to the village, as described in 1540, was via *'a greate stone bridge over the Avon consisting of eight fayre arches'*. A few Barford properties, such as Watchbury, South of Saint Peter's and The Gables, are known to date from this period but most of the surviving timber-framed dwellings date from the 1600s.

Watchbury House

"I have told you about the great age of the house and of the huge oak beams with which it had been made. The floorboards on the first floor were remarkable for their enormous width and thickness. They stretched the length of the long bedroom which Betty and I occupied. Over the years they had warped so that, although they were still as strong as originally, walking on them was rather like going up hill and down dale. Mother kept them well waxed. There were no carpets, just a few rugs and they made an excellent slide. We had fine times sliding up and down the room when Mummy was out, no doubt!"

South of St Peter's

The Gables

Cottages

In the 1600s, most buildings were cramped with 'wattle and daub' construction, thatched roofs and little in the way of creature comforts.

Under attack and carving up the land

The Civil War, culminating in the Battle of Edgehill in 1643, left its small mark on the village. The sturdy, buttressed tower of St Peter's Church still bears the marks of cannon shot fired by Cromwell's Roundheads as they marauded through the village and attempted to shoot down the Royalist flag flying from its summit.

In 1763, the open fields were enclosed and the land allocated to wealthy farmers. From then on, the parish began to take on its present day appearance. Many villagers lost their source of food production, so 'allotments' of land provided the means for some ordinary people to grow their own food and keep livestock such as chickens and pigs. Pigs were a very good way of recycling waste food, including the dregs from the many beer houses, and grew very quickly. The Watchbury Estate was known as Lodge Farm until the middle of the 19th century.

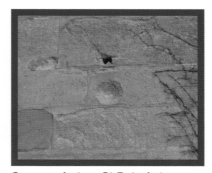

Cannon shot on St Peter's tower

17th century carving of a wool merchant in Watchbury House

Barford School – the beginning

John Beale, the wealthy miller, set up a charitable trust and left £60 in 1672 for *'the purchase of lands, the rent from which was to be put towards the maintenance of a free school in Barford'*. Barford School dates back to 1677, when the Rector and former Headmaster of Warwick School, Thomas Dugard, left £5 a year, £4 of which paid the salary of *'such person as shall teach 14 poor children and the other £1 to teach 2 poor girls'*.

In 1787, the present school house was obtained on a lease and in 1819 was bought by the Reverend Francis Mills for the exclusive use of the schoolmaster. *'The school is kept in the schoolhouse and consists of 30 boys and 30 girls. They are instructed in reading, writing and arithmetic; the girls are taught to sew by the master's wife.'* Clearly, sewing, for girls, was of prime importance.

Church Street

Schoolhouse

Horse power

For many years, horses provided the power for ploughing, harvesting and transport.

The Joseph Arch Pub, formerly the The Red Lion Inn, was a coaching inn for centuries as it was on a main turnpike route

The smell of freshly baked bread would have been wonderful coming from the delivery carts of West's Bakery

Bill Inson as a child on a shire horse with Grandad

The watermill shown here appears to date from about 1800. We know the names of the millers, such as Oldham, from the 1840s.

Fine houses

The late eighteenth and early nineteenth centuries saw the building of several mansions such as Barford Hill House, The Red House, The Glebe, Ivy House, Avonside and Barford House and large extensions added to Watchbury. These were often built by gentry and wealthy property developers. The Quakers were well represented in the village as the Red House and Watchbury had owners who belonged to this movement. Was this to become an influence on Elizabeth Gaskell who attended Miss Byerley's school at Barford House in the early 1820s? Many years later she wrote a short novel 'Lois the Witch', which highlighted religious intolerance. Part of this story is set in Barford and features the drowning of a witch with her cat tied around her neck in the mill pond.

Avonside

Red House

Barford Hill House

Barford House

St Peter's Church

1845 saw fundamental alterations to St Peter's Church when the nave and chancel were completely rebuilt and enlarged and a fine organ installed.

Harvest festival, late 19th century

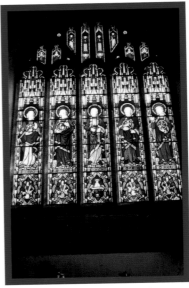

Barford Church, east window

Gates of St Peter's Church
with lamps lit by locally
produced gas or electricity

Chapels

About this time the non-conformist movement had really taken off and the village had both Wesleyan, built in 1840, and Primitive Methodist chapels – both now private dwellings.

"As I have said earlier, when I was 11, we all left the Anglican Church because we did not seem to be on the same 'wavelength' as the old Vicar there. We knew the dear man who ran the tiny Wesleyan Chapel opposite our house, and we decided to go there to worship. We never regretted it. What a difference – we were now 'at home' there and there was genuine warmth and friendship from all who attended. There was a nice harmonium, but no one to play it, so Mother became the organist for the services, and I for the Sunday School. When Mother was absent, I played three times each Sunday. I also took a class, though what I taught the children, I cannot think, but I do know that I loved them and do know they taught me."

SUNDAY SCHOOL TEA.—On Wednesday evening a very nice tea was given to the children belonging to the Wesleyan Sunday School, through the kindness of Mr. and Mrs. W. Harrison, of Sherbourne. About forty six children were present together with about twelve teachers and friends, and a most enjoyable evening was spent. After tea a service of song entitled "Heaven" was very creditably rendered by the children, Mr. C. W. Hunt, the superintendent, conducting, and Mr. J. Williams giving the connective readings. Miss Gourley presided at the harmonium, and Mr. W. Harrison contributed two solos, whilst Miss Lees' rendering of "The Gift" was much appreciated. At the conclusion Mr. Endall proposed a vote of thanks to Mr. and Mrs. W. Harrison, and observed that the service of song might well be repeated and others might be helped and encouraged by it.—Mr. H. Thacker seconded, and Mr. C. W. Hunt remarked that special praise was due to the children who had really only met for two practices.—Mr. Harrison, in acknowledging the thanks, expressed the pleasure it gave him to be able to do something for the children. It was not his desire to entice them away from other schools, but to show them that they had a real place in the thoughts of their teachers, and he hoped that through the labours of their Sunday school they would all come to learn of Jesus and His love.—Mr. Endall concluded with prayer, and a most enjoyable evening was thus brought to a close. It is proposed to hold another service of song in about a month's time.

**Wesleyan School Tea
(Warwickshire Advertiser, 2 January 1902)**

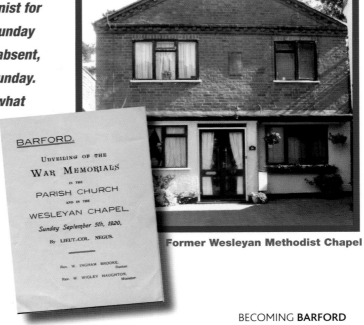

BARFORD.

UNVEILING OF THE
WAR MEMORIALS
IN THE
PARISH CHURCH
AND IN THE
WESLEYAN CHAPEL.

Sunday September 5th, 1920,

By LIEUT.-COL. NEGUS.

Rev. W. INGHAM BROOKE, Rector.
Rev. W. WIGLEY HAUGHTON, Minister.

Former Wesleyan Methodist Chapel

Primitive Methodist Chapel

Joseph Arch, of whom more later, became a charismatic preacher and took his first tentative steps as a 'stirrer up of men' here.

WATCH-NIGHT SERVICES.—Midnight services were held on Tuesday at each place of worship in this parish. At St. Peter's Church a service commenced at 11.30, and consisted of hymns, prayers, and an address by the Rev. S. Parker. At the Primitive Methodist's Chapel the usual two hours' service, consisting of prayers, hymns, and short addresses, was held until New Year's morn; and at the Wesleyan Chapel there was a tea in the evening, given by Mr. Elkington, to all the class members, this being followed by a social gathering, and subsequently by a Watch-night service, conducted by Mr. Elkington, at 11.30. The bells, as usual, rang the Old Year out and the New Year in.

**Warwickshire Advertiser,
4 January 1902**

**Former Primitive Methodist
Chapel, Church Street**

Barford School

By now Barford School was open to all the children of parishioners thanks to the generosity of members of the Mills family. In 1851, the present school was erected by the National Society – a Church of England body. This early school consisted of two large rooms, with boys and girls taught separately. When infants were admitted, part of the Malt Barn opposite was brought into use. Parents had to pay a weekly amount for every child which for some poorer families would have been quite a struggle.

Church Street including old school building

The Malt Barn

1851 school building - now a nursery

Village at work

Barford in the mid 19th century was a largely self-sufficient community. In the 1850s, trade directories of the village list five maltsters, five shoemakers, five carpenters, three tailors, a saddler, a wheelwright, a coachbuilder, a cooper making barrels, a basket and sieve-maker, a cattle doctor, etc. There were also two blacksmiths' forges in Barford. Keytes Lane was deservedly named after the extensive Keyte family most of whom were carpenters and joiners. In 1841 there were 7 such families with 33 members. Thomas Keyte carved the elaborate door of Sun Cottage in Church Street and another Thomas Keyte almost certainly helped to carve the Wellington Memorial in St Paul's Cathedral, London, using his small son as a model for the cherubs.

SOME BARFORD TRADES LISTED IN THE TRADE DIRECTORY OF 1850

Academics Jane Loveday, Jane Rose, Charles Thomas
Butchers Thomas Lees, Sarah Smith
Carpenters Elizabeth, Thomas and Joseph Keyte, John Maylins, Thomas Mills, Nicholas Wright
Farmers John Arkell, W.Canning, Thomas Clark, W. Reading, John Rich, Mark Savage
Gardeners William Carter, John and Richard Hadley, William Hinson
Painters and glaziers William Keyte, James Middleton
Inns, taverns George Inn, J Sharpe, Red Lion, Thomas Clarke
Beer houses William King, Harris Pearson
Maltsters Thomas and Henry Cooke, William King, Thomas Lees, John Sharpe, William Smith
Shoemakers Thomas Clarke, Joseph Hemming, William Hough, William Howard, James Satchwell
Shopkeepers Ann Morris, John Perkins, John Reading
Tailors James and John Hewitt, John Keyte
Blacksmith T. Seeley
Bricklayer J. Sheasby
Seed dealer Ann Smith
Wheelwright John and Richard Taylor

Cottage of saddler and harness maker, opposite Sharpe's Yard

G.HIGGITT SADDLER & HARNESS MAKER

From Inn to butcher's shop

Around 1870, the licence of the George Inn in Bridge Street was terminated for ever with the death of Mary Sharpe who had valiantly taken over the business following the death of her husband, John, nineteen years earlier. Sharpe's Yard was named after these innkeepers.

The premises underwent a dramatic change of use when Mr Ed Hadley bought it and ran it as a butcher's shop. He was also a farmer and there was a stable block at the rear used as an abattoir. Local beasts were slaughtered and butchered at the premises and people could buy back parts of their own animals. Several members of the family continue to be closely involved with the land.

Three generations of the Hadley family

Joseph Arch (1826-1919)

This remarkable man was born, lived and died in a tiny cottage in Barford. Through his oratory, he championed the cause of the impoverished and exploited farm labourers by founding the National Agricultural Workers Union in 1872. Despite leaving school at the age of 9, Arch became an MP and helped get agricultural labourers the vote. He was befriended by The Prince of Wales and the Countess of Warwick and achieved international fame.

Joseph Arch Spy cartoon

Joseph Arch and family, circa 1873

Some notable Barford residents

He was not the only MP to live in Barford during the 19th century. Charles Mills, Edward Greaves, Brooke Robinson and John Stratford-Dugdale occupied some of the larger houses in the village in stark contrast to Arch's humble cottage.

As the new arrivals to Barford in the early nineteenth century built impressive mansions and changed the landscape of the village, the last of the old gentry were leaving for a new life in Australia. John Fairfax was born in Barford in 1804. In 1828, he founded the Leamington Spa Courier. In 1838, he emigrated to the new colony in Sydney, Australia and bought the Sydney Morning Herald, founding a huge publishing dynasty which exists to this day.

John Fairfax

Joseph Arch with grandchildren on holiday

Parish Council matters

Before 1894, the village was governed locally via Parish Meetings.

A Parish Meeting was held at the School Room Barford on Tuesday the 4th December 1894 at 6.30pm.
Mr John Stratford Dugdale QC. of Avonside House took the Chair accordingly. The following were the nominations for the Parish Council: **Bacon** Alfred – Plumber, **Gourlay** James – Estate Bailiff, **Hemmings** James Edward – Baker, **Ivens** William – Agricultural Labourer, **Newberry** Thomas – Farmer, **Partridge** Edward Samuel – Agricultural Labourer.
The Chairman declared all the nominations to be valid.

Minutes of the Parish Council Meeting held in the School room Barford on Wednesday the 19th December 1894 at 6.30pm.
Present Messrs Newberry, Bacon, Hemmings, Ivens, Partridge and Gourlay who made the statutory declarations. Mr Gourlay was elected vice Chairman on the motion of Mr Gourlay and seconded by Mr Ivens. Mr Bacon and Mr Burgess were appointed overseers of the poor up to the 15th April next and Miss Archer Assistant Overseer. Mr Ivens laid on the table the following Resolutions, which he proposed to bring forward at the next meeting of the Council; I For the better management of our School. II The reassessment of Rates for the whole Parish. III Obtaining all documents relating to the Earl Warwicks Charity. IV To see that all footpaths other than High Ways are in good preservation.

Signed R W Lindsay   11th March 1895

Eleanor Archer

Eleanor Archer was a friend of Joseph Arch and lived in his cottage for a number of years while he was at Westminster. She was appointed Assistant Overseer of the Poor for Barford in 1894 and held this post for 30 years. Unusually for a woman at this time, she was also responsible for the census collection and was a reporter for a local newspaper. She had a keen interest in the improvement of mankind in general and the lives of women in particular. Miss Archer was summoned to appear before the all male Barford Parish Council on several occasions to explain her actions.

Eleanor Archer

Georgina Brackenbury was a leading member of the suffragette movement. She was also an accomplished portrait painter, famous for her painting of Emmeline Pankhurst, leader of the suffragette movement.

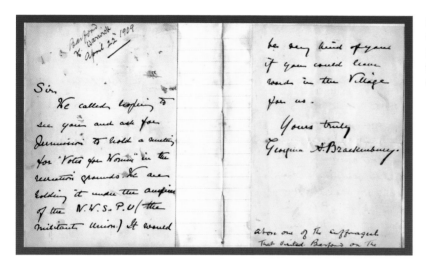

Note from Georgina Brackenbury to the Parish Council

Extract from the Table of Benefactors in St Peter's Church 'There is £5 a year paid by the Earl of Warwick in respect of an ancient right of way in Warwick Park which money is laid out in COALS, for the use of the Poor of this Parish' March 25th 1848

Parish Council Meeting January 16th 1901

'The Clerk reported that he had received £5 from the Warwick Castle Estate and with the £5 received last year it would now be distributed to the cottagers in Barford, one hundred in number.'

Barford gasworks

The village was fortunate in having its own gas works, established in 1872 on the present Bremridge Close (formerly Oldham's) site. This provided fuel for domestic use as well as street lighting. It finally closed in 1920.

"Oh, life was different when I was a girl. In the mornings before I went to school in the village I delivered my grandmother's milk to everybody up the Wellesbourne Road, from the gasometer down as far as Sheasby's. I remember the gas holder there. I used to help the man in charge throw the coke in; he used to let me stand back and he got a great shovel. He would get up at four in the morning. When I went he'd been up several hours. Particularly on Sunday he had to get up early because everybody was doing their cooking and they depended on the gas."

Aerial view of gas works site showing footprint of gasholder

George Worrall, master farrier, at anvil

The Worrall family

Before the motor car, the blacksmith was a key figure in any rural community. He mended farm implements, shoed horses and sometimes repaired cart wheels. In Barford three generations of the Worrall family were village blacksmiths.

Beer

All this hard physical work, coupled with unsafe drinking water, led to a demand for fermented refreshment – usually beer. Barford, as in much of the surrounding countryside, has for centuries had a plethora of malt houses and 'micro breweries'. There were about 13 taverns in the village by the end of the 19th century. Today only 2 of these inns remain.

Carvings above The Wheatsheaf Inn, were they the landlord and landlady?

Row of High Street cottages. The Wheatsheaf Inn was at the far end.

The George Inn

Granville Arms, Wellesbourne Road

Harbury House, formerly the Lord Nelson

The Jones Family who lived in Harbury House

Thomas Hill, landlord of The Red Lion and family

The Red Lion Inn which was renamed The Joseph Arch in 1960

Cedar House

Cedar House was bought in 1870 by Louisa Smith-Ryland when it was renamed The Coffee House. It was widely regarded as one of the finest in the County. Was it at one time The Temperance Hotel mentioned in trade directories? It certainly later became the Barford Club and Reading Room and by the 1950s it housed the popular Barford Working Men's Club.

"whose only fault, if it can be called such, is that it promotes such a strong brand of companionship that many men spend the majority of evenings away from home!"

Louisa Ann Ryland

Notice the windows of Cedar House which were bricked up in the late 18th century to avoid payment of window tax

Milling

1905 saw the beginning of a 'milling dynasty' at Avonside watermill whereby 3 successive generations of Hemmings ran the business. James Hemmings was a farmer, who owned the village store and a bakery. The mill meant he could grind his own corn, bake and sell fresh bread to the locals. He was succeeded by Richard and eventually by David who used the mill to produce animal feedstuffs. In 1916 Barford Electric Company installed equipment at the mill to generate electricity for streetlights and some households. Later the mill became unsafe.

"We enjoyed going to see the Miller and to watch all the great wooden cogs and the enormous water wheel moving together so wonderfully. We saw the flour pouring into bins and sacks and vats. The Miller was always covered from head to foot with flour. One day the whole village was thrown into deep gloom when the news broke that the Miller had been caught up by his coat in the machinery and killed. We were horrified and even today I shudder when I see a big wooden water wheel beside a mill."

The Hemmings family

Farming

The land has played a pivotal role in the life of this rural community with several farms and associated dairies being part of large estates. Unusually, there were two farms right at the heart of the village – Elliot's and Carter's. Both had dairy herds and milk was sold first in open cans and later in bottles.

BARFORD.

BARFORD HILL CREAMERY.—We are very pleased to see that Mr. Smith-Ryland's Creamery at Barford Hill has again come to the front with its produce at the dairy show, held last week at the Agricultural Show, London. In Class 36—for six cream cheeses made from pure cream only—the Creamery was awarded second prize. In this class there were twenty-one competitors, representing creameries from England, Ireland, and Wales. In Class 65—for cream other than clotted, in four pots, the total not to exceed 3lbs.—there were twenty-eight exhibitors, representing nineteen dairies or creameries from all parts of the United Kingdom. Mrs. M. Reading was awarded second prize in this class also. Mrs. M. Reading, as manageress, is to congratulated on doing so well. The Warwickshire County Council is also to be congratulated on Mrs. Reading's success, as she is a pupil they sent to the Dairy School at Kingston, near Derby, a few years ago. Mr. Smith-Ryland's Creamery at Barford Hill received an order a short time ago from Messrs. Lisseter and Miller, Bennetts Hill, Birmingham, to supply cream cheeses for his Majesty's luncheon marquee at the opening of the Birmingham water works at Rhayader, and a letter was afterwards received expressing thorough satisfaction with the cheeses sent.

Leamington Spa Courier 1899

"Sometimes I used to be sent to the dairy up the street to collect milk in a tin can with a handle, but no lid. It was fun to swing it round and round at arm's length and not spill a drop. Then there was skimmed milk to be fetched for cake making. This was topped with up to two inches of froth, but not by the time I got it home - it had been scooped out with a small crooked finger and eaten."

Carter's fields

Carter's fields, beside Keytes Lane, were later to become the recreation ground or 'Rec'. His dairy was in Bridge Street.

Carter's Barn, Bridge Street

Carter's fields where Fairfax Close is now situated

Mechanisation

With the coming of mechanisation, dependence on horses declined. Now, some vehicles were steam-powered. Coal was burned to generate the steam from a water filled boiler. It is thought that the old pumps with the high level spout, set at regular intervals along the roadside, were probably used to refill these water tanks.

Barford Hill Fire Engine powered by steam

Mr Taylor with steam powered dredger used to dredge the Avon

Water pump

Agriculture

Agriculture too was much less labour intensive than in former times. In the 20th century, carriers began to use motorised transport. Commercial garages arrived in Barford and a few private cars and coaches began to appear. Oldham's Transport was originally started using the newly built premises of a former wheelwright in Bridge Street to set up a tractor business. He and his engineer later designed and constructed the first truck for transporting livestock. In time the firm expanded, switched to domestic removals and HGV maintenance and moved to a site on the Wellesbourne Road at the edge of the village. The firm has now relocated and the site has been developed for commercial and residential purposes.

"Many years ago when Guy Oldham saw a herd of cows on their way back to market, thin and dusty after two days travel on the roads, he had the bright idea of transporting them by a quicker method. So he put a box on a van and that is how the business of Oldham's Transport was born. Later the business was taken over by British Road Services. In the 1950's Guy Oldham used to live in Forge Cottage where it is thought that the first all metal plough was invented."

Bremridge's petrol pump

Oldham's cattle trucks

Hemmings Mill

The Barford Electric Company based at the old watermill had vanished without trace by 1927. By this time, with the advent of mechanisation, it was no longer necessary to rely on water power to process the grain. Accordingly, in 1924, animal feed production transferred to newly built premises off Mill Lane. The southern end of The Red Lion had to be demolished so that Red Lion Lane could be widened to take lorries. The business thrived and was a great source of local employment.

The Merry Millers football team

The Great War 1914-1918

The idealism and patriotism shown by so many young, and some not so young, men of Barford who enlisted is humbling. Especially poignant are the pencilled crosses beside those who didn't return. With six million at the front, the Board of Agriculture launched the Land Army in 1915 and by the end of 1917 there were more than a quarter of a million women working on the land.

Abbassia, Cairo

Worrall in Egypt

Leaving for the desert

List of men who enlisted

Warwickshire Yeomanry with Arthur Workman and Charles Smith-Ryland

Officers in Cornwall

In the Cricket Pavilion there hung a photograph of the 1914 Cricket Team.
One item is self-evident, only a minority wore Whites – their social position was
such that the acquisition of cricketing attire would be beyond their means.
There is a note of sadness in this photograph. Many of the younger men were
in their last season, their cricketing days numbered. Within a year or two they
would be among the 'lost generation' of the First World War. On the Barford War
Memorial are the names of these young cricketers, their lives alas so short.
One Sunday evening while attending Barford Church, the Vicar based his
sermon on the following quotation:

"And when the last Great Scorer comes
To write against your name
He will write not that you won or lost
But how you played the Game."

War memorial
programme

The Winston
family

BARFORD 1914–1919.

In memory of those from this Parish
who gave their lives for their
Country in the Great War.

GEORGE MIRONS
JOHN SMITH, M.M.
REUBEN BARNBROOK
ARTHUR HOPKINS.
H. DENNIS SMITH-RYLAND, Capt.
HARRY WOODWARD
FRANCIS B. FREEMAN.
WILLIAM HENRY REEVE.
FRANCIS H. TALBOT.
ALBERT E. WINSTON, L.C.
FREDERICK J. PILKINGTON
WILLIAM CARTER, Cpl.
FREDERICK BARTLETT
C. WISLEY HUNT.
FRANK A. BAKER, L.C.
MARY M. GRAHAM.

"Their name liveth for evermore."

War memorial

School days

Children in the early part of the century frequently left school to take up labouring jobs. The log book of 1928 reports that *"6 boys and 3 girls have left and gone to work during the year and all but one found work easily, mainly of a labouring or domestic nature."* Over the next ten years pupils went into such work as carrier's assistant, farm labourer, domestics, shop assistant and sewing maid. As expectations were low, there was very little social mobility.

Children's health was of great concern in the early 1900s. Encouragingly, in 1926 the School Medical Officer' reported *"Very few defective children found"*. A year later, out of 32 children inspected by the school dentist, 23 required treatment. Measles was a potential killer and a pupil died of rheumatic fever in 1930. Whooping cough epidemics were relatively common and, in 1932, 36 pupils had contracted the disease and the school was closed. In 1937, the District Medical Officer again closed the school as mumps and whooping cough struck. There were also two notifications of diphtheria and the children's books were destroyed. The school reopened with 6 fresh cases of chicken pox! In 1937, The Rural District Sanitary Inspector examined the defective drains in the boys' playground and condemned the whole system as a possible source of disease. No wonder the school nurse visited so regularly and became known as the 'health visitor'.

Barford School children

"When I was six and my sister Beryl seven, we caught diphtheria, as did two teenage girls, one of whom helped my mother in the house. I learned years later that their brother, who was in the navy at Portsmouth, had brought the infection to the village but fortunately it spread no further. We were taken to the local fever hospital, Heathcote (now the Rehabilitation Hospital) and were allowed no visitors the whole time we were there. This was a traumatic experience for small children and several young patients died while we were there. Our local GP, Dr George Tibbets from Warwick, diagnosed the disease by its distinctive odour as soon as he came into the bedroom. In those days patients had complete bed rest so, when we did return home, we were pale and weak and could hardly walk. Luckily we survived the ordeal."

Certificate of exemption from education

Barford School May Day 1912

Barford School scarf drill

Barford School drill

May Day celebration

It was not all work and illness and the young people had opportunities to enjoy themselves and show off their expertise to appreciative audiences.

Social life

In the first half of the twentieth century, television wasn't widely available so villagers made most of their own entertainment. Competitions were very popular.

WARWICKSHIRE ADVERTISER & LEAMINGTON GAZETTE, SATURDAY, OCTOBER 5, 1901.

BARFORD.

LECTURE ON GARDENING.—We are pleased to hear that Mr. Dunkin's opening lecture on gardening was well attended on Wednesday night, an audience of about seventy being present. It is hoped that still more will show their appreciation of both Mr. Dunkin's help and the Technical Education Committee's scheme of placing that help in their midst.

CLERICAL CHANGES.—We regret to learn that the time is fast approaching when the Rev. Douglas Long will be severing his connection with Barford. We believe his curacy terminates in about a fortnight's time, but he will remain in the parish as curate-in-charge until the arrival of the new Rector, about the middle of November next. The successor of the Rev. Cecil Mills is the Rev. W. Sackville Parker, who comes from Rothwell Vicarage, near Kettering. Many of the older parishioners (says a correspondent) will experience keen regrets over the departure of their old friend and rector from the village; and Mr. Long's going away will be as sincerely felt, for during his residence amongst us he has been most sociable and kindly towards all, and has in many ways shown a true interest in the welfare of the parishioners, whose heartiest good wishes are sure to follow him.

MARROW AND POTATO SHOW.—At the Granville Arms, by the kind permission of Mr. E. Boote, the first vegetable marrow and potato show was held on September 27th and the following day. It proved a thorough success. Five Barford and two Wasperton working men formed themselves into a working committee, and from the first meeting to the date of the show was about fourteen days, but considering the short notice the working men of the three villages quickly got together the best and finest collection of vegetable marrows and general garden produce that had ever been shown in the village. It is hoped to make it an annual affair, and also to give the members at least three months' notice previous to the show being held. With the assistance of a few friends by way of donations the committee were able to make out a very good schedule of prizes. Fifteen prizes in all were distributed to the value of £2 5s., ranging from 2s. 6d. to 5s. The exhibits were divided into seven classes, viz., four for vegetable marrows, two for potatoes, and one for a collection of vegetables of six distinct varieties. All the classes were very keenly contested, the collections being exceptionally good. There were fifty-three entries for the different classes. About a hundred and thirty visitors attended, and were loud in their praises of the way the show was managed and also the fine collection of vegetables. Mr. R. Jones, gardener to Mr. Smith-Ryland, of Barford Hill, and Mr. T. Keen, gardener to Mrs. Francis Williams, Watchbury House, were the judges. They gave the committee great credit for their work and also to the members for their fine collections. The tables were very prettily decorated, for which the best thanks of all are due to Mrs. E. Boote and Miss Page. The show was financially a success. The committee consisted of the following: Mr. A. H. Bass, Mr. J. Bartlett, Mr. T. Castle, Mr. C. Keightley, Mr. E. Keyte, Mr. W. West, and Mr. W. Irens (hon. secretary).

HARVEST THANKSGIVING SERVICES.—On Sunday last the annual services of thanksgiving for the ingathering of the harvest were held at St. Peter's Church. There were four services during the day, including two celebrations of the Holy Communion, all the services being conducted by the Rev. Douglas Long, curate of St. Peter's. The collections taken were in aid of the Warneford Hospital, and amounted to £4 11s. 3d. Mr. J. C. Bryan was at the organ, and at both morning and evening services the anthem "He watereth the hills " (by Caleb Simper) was efficiently rendered by the choir. The solos were taken by Mr. Harry Pratt and Mr. Edmund Keyte. The church decorations were the work of

many willing hands, and were quite up to the usual standard of good taste. The chancel was beautifully decked with flowers, adiantum ferns, and corn by Mr. R. Jones and his under gardeners from Barford Hill. The east window was the work of Mr. Keen, of Watchbury. The pulpit was decorated with wheat and cut flowers by the Misses Ayres; the gas standards throughout the church were arranged artistically with cut flowers and honesty plant by Miss Gertie Walton and Miss Badham. The font was arranged with flowers and fruits, including some fine bunches of grapes from the Misses Ayres, whilst the several window-ledges were festooned with trailing ivy around various samples of vegetables. Many thought the church had never looked better, and material for decoration was willingly given by all those already alluded to. In addition Mr. Harry Pratt and Mr. Willie Hunt sent bread in the form of two enormous " twists "; Mrs. T. Sheasby gave some honey; flowers came from Mr. R. W. Lindsay, and grapes from the Misses Ayres. Others who assisted in the decorations on Saturday last, besides those mentioned, were Mrs. Knibb, Miss Bessie Gourlay, Miss L. Hadley, and Mrs. Lewis, from Kilburn, London. There was one of the largest of congregations at the evening service, at which the Rev. Douglas Long preached a suitable harvest sermon. After the service many walked round the church to look at the decorations, and the large collection of vegetables grouped by Mr. J. Wells and Mr. Putnam around the organ received a great deal of attention.

PROFESSOR BLACKIE'S LITANY.

From Professor Blackie's Day-Book, a volume full of good things, we quote the following sentences:—

From a scholar who smells of books, from a sportsman who smells of horses, and from a mother who smells of babies.

Good Lord, deliver me!

From the three infallibles, the Roman Pope, the editor of a party newspaper, and a woman when she is in the wrong,

Good Lord, deliver me!

From a fair woman when she weeps, from a false woman when she smiles, and from a clever woman when she talks,

Good Lord, deliver me!

The whole of his petitions he calls " Litania Nigelli," in jesting reference to his name.

Extract from a villager's scrap-book

"In October 1901 there was a marrow and potato show at The Granville Arms by kind permission of Mr E. Boote. It was the first vegetable, potato and marrow show to be held there."

A much used venue was the Ryland Hall set at the rear of the Arts and Crafts dwelling in Church Street, modestly named 'The Cottage', and built in 1900 for Mrs E. Smith-Ryland. Activities there included Barford Drum and Fife Band, the Choral Society, Scouts, drama productions, concerts, cookery classes, film shows and bridge parties. It was demolished in 1923.

In 1911, a newspaper account of one of the choral society performances reported: *"Miss Roberts contributed 'Rejoice Greatly' from Handel's Messiah. This is a piece of some difficulty, technically somewhat beyond her powers".*

" THE SHADOW OF THE CROSS."—A religious service on the second allegory, " The Shadow of the Cross," by the Rev. William Morris, illustrated with lime-light pictures photographed from life, was conducted in the Schoolroom by the Rev. W. S. Parker, on Monday evening last, for women, and on the following evening for men. The following sacred songs were song, and each illustrated by lime-light lantern : " The Holy City " (Adams), Mrs. S. Tomlinson ; " He was despised " (Handel), Miss E. Staunton ; " Nazareth " (Gounod), Mr. Percy Carter. At the end of each service a collection was made. The services were much enjoyed, and have not been the first of the kind in the village, for during the winter several have been given by Mr. Parker in the schoolroom and have proved helpful and refreshing to the lives of the people. Last month a subject taken was the Epiphany of our Lord. The service was held first for the children and repeated for adults, and the chief events represented on the screen were those suggested by the gospels and special lessons for the feast of the Epiphany and the Sundays in the Epiphany season, viz.: The visit of the wise men from the east, Jesus with the doctors in the temple, the baptism of our blessed Saviour, the first miracle at Cana in Galilee, the healing of the leper, the stilling of the tempest, the cure of the Gardarene demoniac, the sower and the tares, the destruction of the sacred city, and the great day of judgment.

Lime-light pictures

"There were lovely concerts in the village – all local talent, of course. The Smith-Rylands allowed us to use their 'Ryland Hall' which they used for private parties and the occasional Ball. It was beautifully equipped with a fine stage, good curtains and dressing rooms."

RYLAND HALL CINEMA,
BARFORD.

Easter Monday,
At 7-30 p.m.

Our great EASTER TREAT to BARFORD

TOM   MIX,
in
"Roaring Reform."
Even Better than "Wilderness Trails."
recently shewn.
IN FIVE PARTS.

ALICE   HOWELL
in
"BEHIND THE FRONT,"
TWO-REEL   COMEDY.

ONE - MAN   BAND.

PRICES :   8d. and 1/3 (including Tax).
Children· Half-Price.

T. J. Kennard, Printer, Leamington.

The rifle range

The Miniature Rifle Range was built at the turn of the century. As well as .22 rifle shooting it was also used for the Scouts, St John's Ambulance Brigade, whist drives and dances and always a flower and vegetable show. It was demolished in the 1950's when it was said to be one of the oldest surviving ranges.

"We didn't really have a village hall as such. We used to use the rifle range which was down by the bridge. It was quite a rough place in comparison to the Ryland Hall, but quite clean".

Barford Rifle Club

Miniature Rifle Club, 1924

St John's Ambulance

"I was beginning to love to dance now and I went as often as my mother allowed me to the Rifle Club dances. All the boys and girls met there and had a fine time dancing to Syd Dean's music. I was 16 and had a knee length, pink crepe-de-chine dress, stockings and black dancing pumps".

The Women's Institute

Soon after peace was declared, the Women's Institute was started in Barford. Since 1919, the members have maintained a formidable and effective presence to the present day.

"My mother joined the Women's Institute and learned a great deal: how to use all the things in the garden to the best advantage, how to cure rabbit skins, make baskets, dressmaking. She made a fine muff with rabbit skin. It was so well done that she won first prize – an inlaid mahogany tea tray."

Women's Institute outing, 1925

Barford Memorial Hall

Barford Memorial Hall was given to the village in 1931 by Mrs Leila Smith-Ryland in memory of her husband, Charles Ivor Smith-Ryland. In 1952, the land was given to the Parish Council by Charles M. T. Smith- Ryland to be held in trust for the village *"for the purpose of physical and mental training and recreation and social, moral and intellectual development of the inhabitants of the Parish of Barford without distinction of sex, political, religious or other opinions."* The Memorial Hall has been a much used venue for a wide range of village activities ever since.

Barford Memorial Hall welfare clinic

The British Legion outside Barford Memorial Hall

Royal visit

1935 was the year of King George V's Jubilee. It was an occasion for much rejoicing in the village. The school was closed, homes were bedecked with flags and street parties held.

Prince of Wales visits Barford

The playing field

In 1938, the King George V Jubilee Trust Fund enabled the present playing field to be acquired as a permanent open space for the village. The land had to be thoroughly ploughed and levelled to get rid of the 'ridge and furrows.' By natural justice this land should have been made available to the village about 40 years earlier. The Parish Council minutes of 1894 show that Lord Warwick's offer of the field was rejected out of hand following letters of objection from the influential owners of Watchbury and Barford House!

Witches Hat roundabout – great fun but removed due to health and safety concerns

Recreation

Barford in the 1930's had its own football team, cricket side, bowling club and miniature rifle club. Young people were able to join the Wolf Cubs or Brownies, Guides or Scouts, one of the church youth groups or choir.

Barford Cubs with Lady Howard

Brownie house

Barford Guides, 1932

Scouts at Barford Hill boathouse

Barford Cricket team, 1929

Second World War– helping the war effort

A public meeting was held in March 1941 to implement the Government Scheme for Preservation of Fruit. At this meeting it was decided to form a centre and a committee. The Canning Dept was at Mrs Guy Oldham's, at the forge. Mrs Inson's, Wellesbourne Road, was also used.

"Oh, do you all remember the WI canning in Inson's Yard? Every village was encouraged to do this for the war effort. When fruit was in season, pears, plums and that, a group of women got together preparing the fruit and putting it in cans with sugar syrup. The lids were put and sealed by a machine provided by the Government, the cans were put in a big net and carefully lowered into the washing copper, which was filled with boiling water. Sometimes tins would explode; this made a mess and sometimes months later a tin could be opened only to find that the fruit was bad due to the tin not being sealed properly."

Women's Institute canners

"We children were allowed out of school to pick blackberries and rosehips for the war effort."

"The Women's Institute President in 1943, Lady Burton, arranged an egg collection in the village for the Warneford Hospital and 120 eggs were sent. This collection continued on a regular basis."

Jim and Ettie

John Smith, baker, inspecting hot cross buns baked on Good Friday over a period of 17 years. They kept well while those baked on Maundy Thursday or Easter Saturday did not.

"It was a dreadful night, 14th November 1940, I'll never forget it. I got up at my usual time about 3.00 am and started work. We managed to get the bread made and delivered with none to spare. We were just having a cup of tea in the bake-house, when Lady Burton arrived to ask if we could take some bread to Coventry – the city was without bread and the water supply was shattered. Even though we had been up all night we got the oven going. The following morning we headed towards Coventry, loaded up with 400 loaves and 50 gallons of water. The police let us through and when the women saw what we had, they hugged and kissed us, lifted us up and wept."

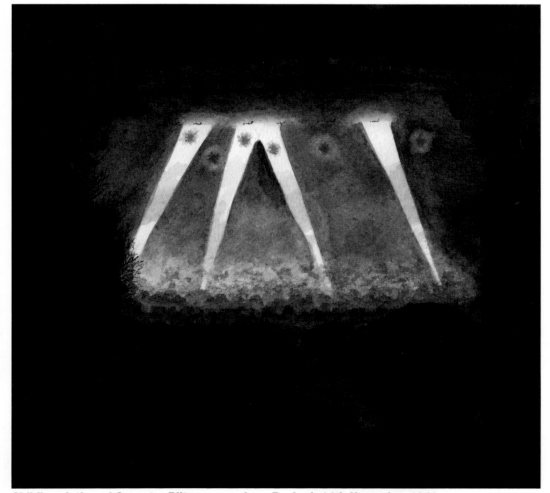

Child's painting of Coventry Blitz as seen from Barford, 14th November 1940

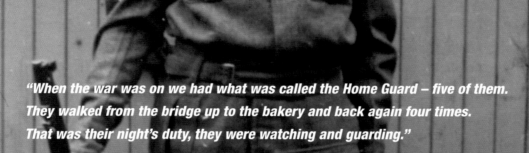

"When the war was on we had what was called the Home Guard – five of them. They walked from the bridge up to the bakery and back again four times. That was their night's duty, they were watching and guarding."

"The village home guard was formed with strict discipline applied. Members were required to do a total duty of 48 hours in four weeks. For failing to attend Parade the maximum penalty was £10 or a month's imprisonment when not mustered. A Pill Box sited at Barford Bridge was manned and an incident occurred. Whilst on duty, three rounds of rifle ammunition were fired at a rabbit in the meadow, but missed. This was a serious misuse of ammunition and resulted in a full enquiry being held. Compulsory drills and training ended September 1944. The Home Guard stood down in December 1944."

Wartime wedding

County of Warwick.

Air Raid Precautions Scheme.

This is to Certify that

Miss A. C. WALL,

of 2, Keytes Lane, Barford,

has completed a course of Anti-Gas Training held under
the auspices of the Warwick Rural District Council
and has acquired sufficient knowledge of Anti-Gas Measures
for personal protection.

Nature of Course attended Voluntary Aid Course.
Name and qualification of Instructor E. Arthur Lyne, C.A.G.S.
                                    Signed

Date 9th October, 1938.   Hon. Organiser.

NOTICE   FN 259830

1. Always carry your
Identity Card. You must
produce it on demand by a
Police Officer in uniform or member of H.M. Armed Forces
in uniform on duty.

2. You are responsible for this Card, and must
not part with it to any other person. You must
report at once to the local National Registration Office if
it is lost, destroyed, damaged or defaced.

3. If you find a lost Identity Card or have in your
possession a Card not belonging to yourself or anyone in
your charge you must hand it in at once at a Police
Station or National Registration Office.

4. Any breach of these requirements is an offence
punishable by a fine or imprisonment or both.

FOR AUTHORISED ENDORSEMENTS ONLY

T 51/2878/1

NATIONAL
REGISTRATION
IDENTITY
CARD

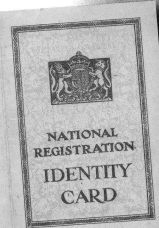

**Mary Winningham, in
fancy dress, 'dig for
victory'**

Night of confusion. Ada's story

"Mother had lit a fire under the copper when she spotted a face, followed by a body that slithered down the wall into a heap in the yard. She was convinced he was the German from the plane that crashed because all night long all she could hear was the sound of the Home Guard running up and down the street, whistles blowing, a real commotion going on. So she grabbed her copper stick and hit this poor man across the back of the head and knocked him out. She ran down the village looking for someone from the Home Guard. Mr Workman turned the man over and said "For Christ's sake Ada, what have you done? This is the man from Coventry Home Guard. They are here with a battalion helping us!"

Land Army girls

In 1940 the Women's Land Army was formed with 110 members throughout Warwickshire, of whom a number were in Barford.

"Land girls were stationed at Barford Hill. I can see them now, a bevy of land girls going down to the pub, the village lads had never seen anything like it.
Some land girls stayed with village families. Helena lodged with Mr & Mrs Benfield in Keytes Lane, and Doreen, another local land girl, married a Barford boy, Bill Freeman."

Land Army, 1945

A few of the fallen

The War was no respecter of persons and officers and men were equally vulnerable to death and injury. By December 1940 there were approximately 520 men of the Royal Warwickshire Regiment who were prisoners of war in Germany.

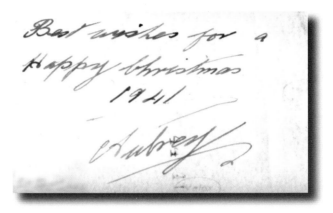

Last poignant message from Aubrey Upstone. He was a nurse on the SS Polyanthus. This ship of the Merchant Navy was torpedoed and he never returned.

Westham House, a C16 timber-framed farmstead later enlarged as a hunting lodge, was home to the Hon. Gustavus Lascelles Hamilton-Russell. He and his brother Hon. Desmond Claud Hamilton-Russell enlisted in the Grenadier Guards and were both killed on active service.

Lawrence Edward Willoughby Byam was the 19 year old son of a distinguished Harley Street doctor who, with his family, came to live in Barford in The Old Mill House to escape the London bombing. He trained for the Fleet Air Arm and his plane was lost at sea.

Westham House

In 1940, the Seaford Ladies College was evacuated from a bombed area of Sussex to Westham House. In 1947, Westham House became a residential college where people from towns were given the chance to study in a rural environment. The college extended its brief to a wide range of activities and studies as an Adult Education Centre.

"I was four at the start of the war when my school was evacuated to a manor house at Barford, Warwickshire. This was definitely traumatic. Catching the train at Paddington each term was awful. I did not wash the spot of my mother's last kiss for some time. We saw the planes in the sky for the raids on Coventry and the thousands of planes going over early in the morning on D-day. There was porridge (often lumpy) and bread and margarine for breakfast. When the first oranges appeared there was great excitement. We all caught every conceivable childhood disease, in spite of being given cod liver oil and malt and all being given syrup of figs every Sunday. We had two baths a week in two inches of water, otherwise cold water for washing. Clean clothes once a week. These included in winter, woollen vests, liberty bodices, woollen stockings with suspenders and long navy knickers and viyella shirts."

Housing

In 1946, many 19th century dwellings were condemned as being unfit for human habitation and there was an urgent need for housing. Warwickshire County Council bought land from St John's College, Oxford and built the mixed development of private and council housing at Sandy Way.

The rats come up from the river and break into the house through the clay and wattle walls. There was only one room. Quite horrible – water from the pump, toilet up the garden, night-soil men coming round – the children shout 'here comes the jam factory!' Tin bath to be hauled in on bath night. No electricity when we first came here, only oil lamps. We got electricity 1945. I used to come down in the night to heat the milk and the cockroaches all came across the floor and I'd have to kill them with a shoe. The pleasure of a thatched cottage!"

Barford School

Barford School was maintained by the Church of England until 1948 when financial responsibility was passed to the County Council. Years later it was to become St Peter's Church of England (voluntary aided) Primary School.

The Glebe Hotel

Also in 1948, the beautiful Georgian Rectory next to the church proved too expensive for the church to maintain and so was sold to Otto Heskey, a refugee from Czechoslovakia. It became the Glebe Hotel.

Boarded up Georgian Rectory

The Glebe Hotel

Rationing

Even in peacetime life was not without problems. The 1950's and '60s could almost be dubbed the decades of demolition and change. Rationing continued into the 1950's although the deprivation was probably less severe in our rural community than in the towns and cities. The children were more concerned with the continuing rationing of sweets.

Allotments

NH 599665

Motor Fuel Ration Book

MOTOR CAR

1501 – 2200 C.C.

14 – 19 H.P.

This book is the property of Her Majesty's Government

The coupons in this book authorise the furnishing and acquisition of the number of units of motor fuel specified on the coupons. Wt. 33559 51-9063

NH 599665

Registered No. of Vehicle	Registered No. of Vehicle
Date and Office of Issue	Date and Office of Issue

Instructions to Issuing Clerk:
See that the issue of this Ration Book is Recorded on the applicant's registration book.

This portion, after completion, to be detached and forwarded to the Regional Petroleum Officer with Form P 2218

Livestock

"We kept pigs and chickens out the back. The pigs were killed by a man outside in the lane. We chopped the pig up and washed out all the chitterlings, then hung it all up in the wash-house."

Bill Worrall with pigs

"Nearly everyone kept a pig. Mr. Arty Wells used to kill the pigs, he arrived with his tools attached to his belt and there it was killed. Straw was lit to burn the bristles off the pig. It was scraped and salt and water were used to cool it down. It was hung on a beam in the scullery where it was opened. Chitterlings were used, lard made from fat and often the chitterlings were taken to large families in the village. The bits of the pig which could not be preserved were shared around with other families, secure in the knowledge that they too had a pig which would be shared out in turn. During the war, at lunch time, many children from the school took basins down to Mr. Hadley, the butcher, to collect hot home-made faggots which he produced in bulk for sale."

Post-war Barford

After the war there was an acute shortage of money, materials and manpower and the problem of maintaining large, draughty mansions without an army of staff became acute. Barford Hill House was demolished in 1954.

Barford Hill House dining room

"I used to have jobs in the big house – grinding coffee, cleaning silver, churning butter in a big tub. Mum was the temporary cook from 1945-50. I used to help my Dad in the stables, catching rats, looking after the ponies and milking the cows. We all had jobs to do, especially in the war, but we had some good times – fun times as well. I remember in the war years we used to go with Charles and his family all over the place such as Cowdray Park for the polo."

Estate workers

C. Tallis, gamekeeper and dog Ben

Estate workers, early 19th century

The Red House (demolished in the 1930's)

"The house is lovely with lots of stone passages. It has a large dining room in the front, a drawing room, a big hall with a curved staircase and lots of fireplaces. There is a large kitchen and scullery with an Aga - it's lovely. There are 3 bathrooms, one with a great big bath. We have the evacuees who are staying in the little cottages in Church Street come up twice a week for a bath – and what a mess they make!"

Rummage Auction Sale, arranged by Mrs. Guy Lea, in aid of Missions to Seamen, in the Memorial Hall, Saturday, December 3rd, at 3 p.m.

Congratulations to Mr. Brian Lea on graduating B.A. (Cambridge) with honours. Mr. Brain Lea has been accepted by the Church Missionary Society for service in Africa. He will help in agriculture, in which he is qualified, and for a year will be gaining practical experience on a farm. He has kindly promised to join Miss Marsh in running the Junior Church and will help the Rector with a Junior Guild for the new Confirmation candidates, over 20 in number. The Lord Bishop has also given special permission for Mr. Lea to help in the Sunday services.

An Anonymous Gift of Markers for the lectern is gratefully acknowledged. More are needed for the Altar and Prayer Desks. Moreover, the Lectern Bible, the Altar Service Book, the Prayer Desk's Service Books, are all tattered and torn. Will anybody like to give the church a Christmas present?

The Fellowship arranged a most enjoyable social and made, moreover, a profit of £8 for the Pageant expenses.

The Harvest Festival congregations, in common with other parishes in this bountiful year, were unusually large, and in the evening nearly filled the 600 seats in our church—easily the largest in the Deanery after Stratford Parish Church. We rejoiced to have Mr. Dunstan with us and he preached three times and again on the Monday at Hertford Hill Hospital, to which the flowers and bread and corn had been taken for their Harvest Thanksgiving. The Choir excelled themselves in the Anthem "The Earth is the Lord's," and the collections amounted to £23. Our grateful thanks for all gifts and help with the decorations.

Youth Guild.—On October 15th, after three months of hard work in converting the Rectory Barn into a new club room, a Harvest Supper was held for members of the Youth Guild and friends who had given materials for decorating the barn.

Mrs. Parr declared the new headquarters open.

We were pleased to have our founder, Mr. Dunstan, present.

The Lamp, 1955

Molly and Guy Lea, last residents of the Red House

Site of the Red House

Time passes

Reason, Booker and West families

Mabel and Annie Reason

Barford in the 1950's

'If anyone wanted to find a village which could be an ambassador for Britain, he could hardly make a happier choice than Barford. For though it may be more urban, than some of its smaller neighbours, it is characterised by a cheerful, bustling liveliness, that is entirely English. There is a phenomenal amount of activity among its estimated 850 inhabitants. Their British Legion, for instance, does not come to life merely on Remembrance Sunday. Frequent are the meetings of a virile group of ex-service men. There is a Working Men's Club with rather more than 150 members. For women there is a Women's Institute, with a membership fluctuating between 80 and 100, and a Mothers' Union attached to the church which constantly organises events to aid funds. Lately, there has been a most successful bazaar, and a nativity play outstandingly beautiful and well-produced. Nor are these clubs all that Barford offers, though the life in them alone reflects the atmosphere of the village. Barford Rifle Club , a curious affair in so small a place, is one of the oldest in the country, having been formed at the turn of the century, and claiming to have the record for the longest unbroken period of existence. Thirty people are in an amateur dramatic society called the Barford Players, which produces regularly under the village schoolmaster, Mr. A.S. Twigger. The positive manifestation of all this activity is in the firmly-built village hall, which is in such demand that an event next April is already on the books. Recently it has been handed over by Capt. Smith-Ryland and Mrs Cartwright to a village trust.'

Living History play, set in the 1950's

Quick, run!

"We went fishing in the boat from the boathouse, scrumping on the allotments and annoying the village policeman. I got into quite a bit of trouble because I was not a good runner and was often left behind!"

Shops

"The butcher's shop was kept by Mr Hadley. He had inherited it from his father, as was the custom, in villages. Mother bought from Mr Hadley the most delicious faggots and pig's fry, this was a mixture of raw liver, lights and fat, absolutely delicious fried. The yard was always indescribably messy with mud, blood and entrails lying about. One day I stepped on a sheep's bladder and was squirted in the face, revolting."

"The children walked to Sherbourne to get milk from Harrisons. The family got coal from Hinsons and their household wares such as saucepans, paraffin and scourers from the hardware van. Everything they needed was close at hand. Indeed the bakehouse sold the tastiest iced buns. Mrs Carter who lived opposite Gladstone Terrace in Church Street, sold wool and haberdashery and next door to her was a shop selling fruit and vegetables. This was Mrs Webb who also sold frozen 'Jubblies' made from orange squash for half a penny."

Bridge Street

Old village shop.
Wellesbourne Road

Hadley's Butchers.
Bridge Street

TEA GARDENS BARFORD.

Steeds garage

Barford at work

B. Bacon and B. Winston at work

Carpenter Mr Green and son

The Barlow family at work with a very young Tim in the driving seat

The first village taxi

Barford milkman Goff Tilling

Blacksmith Bill Worrall

Nurse Davinia

G WORRALL FWCF
FARRIER, BLACKSMITH
AND
RURAL ENGINEER
BARFORD 256

Newspaper boy, Phil Hammond

Barford Drama Group

In 1947 the inaugural meeting of The Barford Players was held in the School and made a good start with some thirty members. Over the next decade productions such as *Quiet Weekend, Count your Blessings, Pink String and Sealing Wax* and *Love in a Mist* were much enjoyed by appreciative audiences. Now named Barford Drama Group, the organisation continues to flourish.

"The Church Social was a great success. The features of the evening were a potato-dressing contest for the ladies, an obstacle race for the gentlemen, and a sketch, The Cat's Cradle, *by Noel Coward, read by two of the Barford Players. Games, dancing and community singing completed the programme. The ladies of the Council conjured some refreshments from somewhere. To all who came, thank you for your support. To those who did not, we shall be glad to see you next time, even if your arrival strains the accommodation. We shall be particularly glad to welcome some of you lads in the late 'teens or early twenties. You will not be short of a partner."*

Bonaventure

Drama group rehearsal with former school headmaster Mr Twigger

Church choir

"I thought it would be a good idea if we could have a girls' choir at church and approached Archdeacon Parr about it. 'Come back when you have found six girls' he said, so half an hour later I came back and the girls' choir came into being, no doubt much to the disgust of the boys. I'm ashamed to say that we were rather badly behaved chatting and giggling in the choir stalls and Mr Allibone, the Organist and Choirmaster, would frown and wag his finger at us in the mirror above the organ. At Christmas we would be driven to large houses on the outskirts of the village where we would sing carols in their beautifully decorated halls and then be rewarded with cups of homemade soup, mince pies and fruit. These were magical experiences for us in a time of austerity, never to be forgotten."

Church choir

Church choir

Church Youth Group, 1955

Pageant of the Nativity

The combined efforts of nearly 100 villagers went into the preparation of the first Pageant of the Nativity in January 1951. It was an all village performance produced by the Harley-Smiths. All who took part were nameless and throughout there was a wonderful spirit of friendliness and cheerful co-operation. This very beautiful act of worship was witnessed by over a thousand people and many stated that they were deeply moved by the simple and reverent way in which the performers interpreted their parts. The Pageant has since become a 5-yearly Barford tradition.

St. Peter's Church
BARFORD

The
Story of Christ's Nativity
Presented in MIME & MUSIC by the
Choir and Parishioners
of

Pageant programme

The first Pageant production team

Pageant, early 1950's

The sporting village

Barford football team

The Meet

Cricket at Hareway Lane

Pastoral idylls

"We all played in the Rec., this is now Fairfax Close. It had a lovely red May tree on the corner and two large walnut trees at the other end of the field. We children would find hard nuts in the long grass under our shoes and take off the outer covering which stained our hands brown. If Mr Boote, the owner, saw us he would chase us off, but we would soon return when he had gone. He was later to leave money, in the form of a charity, to the village."

Picnic on the village green

Hadley family picnic, 1936

Swimming in the Avon at Barford

Village weddings

Three coachloads of people from the village, plus others, made the journey to St Margaret's, Westminster and afterwards to the Savoy Hotel for the marriage of Mr Charles Smith-Ryland with Jeryl Gurdon.

The happy couple

The Village Hall in its wedding finery

Villagers on their way to the wedding reception

Inson's wedding

Village outings

In addition occasional excursions were organised for the village children.

"We don't know yet, where we are going, Mrs 'outing' Taylor hasn't told us. But Mum's been paying into the club every week, so it's going to be a good day. Mrs Outing takes us to the big park on a coach, and in summer we go to the theatre in Coventry to see the Birthday Show. We have also been on a holiday to Clacton, oh it was brilliant. It was last April, it snowed. But we went in the sea every day and had ice cream. Too many, I think, because we spent all our money while we were there."

Picnic in the 1950s

Ready for the outing

Her Majesty's Coronation

"On Trinity Sunday, 31 May 1953, special forms of service have been issued by command of the Queen, and will be used at the 11 am and 6.30 pm services. We invite every villager to be present at these services. Our Queen has sworn to dedicate her life, be it long or short, to the service of her peoples; let us all support her in her tremendous task with our prayers."

"Tuesday 2 June, Coronation Day – The Village Committee has arranged a first-class programme with plenty of fun and games and there will be street parties as well. The Committee has asked that the day begin with a short Service in the Church at 9.30 am, and we hope to welcome young and old on this great and historic day, and we trust that it will be a lifelong memory to the end of their days. It would be nice if all the villagers made the day a stay-at-home family party. There will be something doing in the village all the time."

Planting of the Coronation Oak

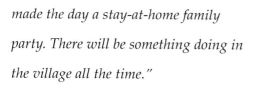

Decorated for the Coronation

Joseph Arch lives on

Red Lion Inn renamed Joseph Arch in the 1960s

Agricultural Workers Union march in Barford, 1967

So, you have come with us on a journey
through time and discovered that Barford is not
just a place on the map but a vibrant community
surrounded by history and beauty –
a village we are proud of.

Barford today

As one of our older villagers writes about the 1930's

'Barford was a small, pretty and very friendly village. You knew everyone and everyone knew you'

This applies as strongly now as then - the sense of support, sociability and being surrounded by friends. This is the true appeal of village life.

Barford Village Shop

Groceries Internet
Coffee Shop Post Office
Fresh Local Produce

Barford landscapes

' For nature gives to every time and season some beauties of its own,

And from morning to night, as from the cradle to the grave,

Is but a succession of changes, so gentle and easy,

That we can scarcely mark their progress'

Nicholas Nickleby by Charles Dickens

Acknowledgements

This book would not have been possible without the very generous grant awarded by the Heritage Lottery Fund and a grant obtained via the Nationwide Building Society Community Award Scheme. Dr. Maggie Hayward and Wendy Barlow worked very hard to secure the £25,000 that has made everything possible. A very sincere 'thank you' goes to the people of the village, past and present, who have allowed us to copy their documents, photographs and house deeds. We gratefully appreciate the help of many people who have chatted to us over a cup of tea and allowed us to record their recollections of village life. Barford Drama Group cooperated with us in our two historical productions and the W.I. kindly organised the catering at various heritage events. Mike Long of Hi-Pix has generously allowed us to use some of his excellent images of the village including the photograph used for the cover. We also gratefully acknowledge the help of many professionals, particularly in the County Record Office at Warwick, the Shakespeare Birthplace Trust Library and Archive at Stratford upon Avon and staff at the Coventry and Birmingham Record Offices who have helped us to discover the past. All these people helped us understand the complexity of old wills and documents, decipher handwriting and strange spelling, and even stranger abbreviations. Their help was invaluable. The staff at the Libraries of Leamington Spa, Warwick, Wellesbourne, Birmingham and Oxford sourced books for us and helped us to unravel the dreaded microfilm so that we could read the old newspapers. We also acknowledge with thanks the editor of the Leamington Spa Courier for permission to publish articles from their titles. Last but not least, we must also thank the members of the Barford Heritage Group who between them have spent countless hours on research and cataloguing of photographs and documents. We would especially like to thank Dr. Chris Hayward for his good humour and patience in allowing his home to be used for our meetings and as a storeroom. This is a picture of Barford through the ages. The authors are well aware that lack of knowledge, time and space has forced us to omit much we would have liked to include. Please forgive any errors or omissions we may have made, your help in improving the situation will always be appreciated.

Compilers/Editorial Team

Maggie Hayward

Wendy Barlow

Carole Whiteley

Ann and Alan McDermott

Graphic Design

Martin Nolan

Publishing Advisor

Phillipa Hayward

Proofreading

Nicky Lawrence

Barford Heritage Group   2005 – 2010

We are now in the final stages of a journey that started in 2005. Since then the group have planned and carried out the following projects:

The creation of a free full-colour heritage trail leaflet 'Bridge to Barford.'

The placing of plaques throughout the village marking significant sites and buildings.

Big screen presentations of the two Heritage Trails.

The recording and transcribing of villager's reminiscences.

Well attended exhibitions that stimulate people to value their heritage, including the mounting of exhibitions for Heritage Open Days.

The development of the Heritage Website; www.barfordheritage.org

The writing of a play, 'Living History,' by villagers (through workshops and editorial groups) using reminiscences collected by the Heritage Group.

The writing and production of a dramatic presentation, 'It happened in Barford,' centred around the life and achievements of Joseph Arch.

The creation of DVD's of the two productions mentioned above.

Lectures/presentations to our village and to other history and heritage groups.

Hosting of visiting groups on tours of the village.

The archiving of information using a variety of methods.

The production of this book using some of the materials and knowledge we have gathered over the years.

The design and production of an exterior display board with village and heritage information.

The production of cards of 'Bygone Barford' for sale.

Barford Heritage Group, 2005 – 2010

Maggie Hayward, *Chairman*, Wendy Barlow, *Treasurer/Reminiscences*, Carole Whiteley, *Project Manager*, Ann McDermott, *Book Secretary*, Alan McDermott, *Photographer/Archivist*, Shirley Osbourne, *Secretary/Transcriber of Reminiscences*, Brenda Barbour, *Creative Designer*, Keith Roberts, *Web Master*, Barbara and Vic Cheshire, Ken Hope, Kirsty Healey, *Researchers*. William Worrall, Elspeth Monks, Sally Hallowell-Carew, Jan Reader, Roger Clay, Jan Bradley, Jean Liggins, Anne Hope, Sue Machado, Barbara Offiler, Peter Wilson, Philippa Mitchell, Catherine White and other people who have contributed to the group over the years.

HERBOR

A R
a R o
39 . 1 . 15

Gravel
Pitt
1 . 0 . 0

Mr Ward's
old
inclosure

Mr Neal

M

A

N

Mr Cockbill

K .

The Revd Mr MILLS.

WARWICK

L .